T0365861

The Mermaid Legends
and the
Maidens of the Sea

Book 2

Poems for Children and
the Young at Heart

JAMES WHITMER

The Mermaid Legends and the Maidens of the Sea Book 2
POEMS FOR CHILDREN AND THE YOUNG AT HEART

iUniverse books may be ordered through booksellers or by contacting:

iUniverse
1663 Liberty Drive
Bloomington, IN 47403
www.iuniverse.com
844-349-9409

ISBN: 978-1-6632-5311-8 (sc)
ISBN: 978-1-6632-5310-1 (e)

Library of Congress Control Number: 2023908560

Print information available on the last page.

iUniverse rev. date: 05/09/2023

Table of Contents

The Mermaid Legends

Book #1: *The Beginning*

2

The Octopus Legends and the Maidens of the Sea

Underneath a midnight moon,
as frogs, and toads, and crickets croon,
sweet maidens of the seven seas,
and swimming in the swaying breeze,
to the mermaid legends listen,
as their sweet eyes glow and glisten,
from an octopus as green
as emeralds in a treasure chest,
and on her head a starfish crest,
as red as rubies, crimson, deep,
which shines and sparkles as she speaks.

And as the midnight moonlight dances
upon these maidens' shining faces,
they listen close in happy trances,
moonbeams in their eyes in traces,
and as these legends do unfold
of sailors lost and treasures old,
of mariners of the seven seas,
of islands neat with colored trees,
of cold and pounding surf and waves,
of tridents lost in deep sea caves,
of yellow birds on beaches where
dragonflies, golden, kiss the air,
of flying fish above the waters,
and diamonds, bright, for sailors' daughters,
these maidens of the reeds and sands,
who wait for ships from far-off lands,
of old sea cats in crow's nests, high,
of salmon-colored evening skies,
of gloomy, hidden, secret caves,
below the rocking, rolling waves,
of starfish swimming 'round in swirls,
their colors bright as mermaids' curls,
of sailors waiting for romance,
as seahorses on the waves, do dance,
of lantern fish in shallow waters,
of praying, hoping, sailors' daughters,

of red clams neat upon the shore,
of sailors' songs and sailors' lore,
that tells where buried treasure rests,
sapphire rings and golden crests,
of moons above and caves below,
of rock crabs crawling ever slow,
of stars in moonless, cloudless nights,
of fancy seabirds full in flight,
of rolling, rocking oceans swelling,
of ships' bells clanging, ringing, knelling,
these bells of copper, polished bright,
and ringing deep into the night,
their desperate, frantic sailors' pleas,
cascading over desperate seas,
of rockfish swimming in the night,
of angelfish in circles, tight,
of treasures lost and treasures found,
of black-red scorpions gone to ground,
of islands neat with palm trees swaying,
of storms and squalls and sailors praying,
of clipper ships and sturdy whalers,
of mermaids and their long-lost sailors,
who wear long strands of mermaid hair,
around their necks with love and care,
of sailors' songs and mermaids' chants,
while pink flamingos, they do dance,
on pebbled beaches white as snow,
with golden starfish as they glow,
of schooners lost in deep, dark storms,
of sea kraits swimming neat in in swarms,
of blue-black whales, eyes dark as coal,
and dolphins, thick, in shoals and shoals,
of purple fronds from purple palms,
of doldrums quiet as the psalms,
of sirens' songs from waters, deep,
that beckon squids from sea swells, steep,
to guide the ships of sailors, lost,
through winter storms and early frost,

of sunken treasures lost at sea,
of silver coins and golden keys,
of wizards and their potions, bright,
of fireflies in the deep, dark night,
that glow and glisten as the waves,
above the deep and darkened caves,
where yellow eels and sea snakes, three,
guard sparkling gems green as the sea,
of seas of wild tempests raging,
of sailors' daughters, waiting, aging,
for ships from far-off seafaring lands,
to safely dock on friendly sands,
of rings of gold and rings of silver,
of silver rain and silver rivers,
of sailors lost in desperate seas,
their voices sharp with desperate pleas,
of gold doubloons and silver strands
of mermaids' hair on sailors' bands
they wear around their necks on voyages,
of golden eels and sea snakes, poisonous,
of red flamingos dancing free,
where sand dollars linger by the sea,
of parrotfish in circles, tight,
that swim in moonless, starless nights,
while damselfish in neat designs,
form deep, dark, perfect, even lines,
of castles, dark, where sea snakes nest,
and guarding jewels in treasure chests,
of arctic terns on whales' backs,
of sea spiders colored red and black,
and in their webs are deep, blue pearls
that shine as bright as mermaids' curls.

These maidens of the seven seas,
these sea nymphs listen for the pleas,
of sailors lost in waters, cold,
of gallant sailors, brave and bold,
their eyes as bright as polished gold.

These sea maids' sparkling eyes do flash,
just as the purple waves do crash,
and in their hearts they keep these legends,
ancient tales that they've been told,
and whispered neat in calming tones,
and by an octopus of old,
and told with reverence, duly blessed,
and while their gentle, maiden fingers,
to their lovely lips are pressed.

BOOK 2: *The Maidens of the Seven Seas*

The Mermaid *Amarantha* and the Twilight on the Waves

When the moon is looming low,
when twilight lingers near,
when starfish with their colors bright,
they pray for moonbeams to appear.

When damselfish, their spots snow white,
when taimen swim in pairs,
it is then that little mermaids,
to the brightly, glowing heavens
softly say their evening prayers.

The mermaid *Amarantha* knows,
each little mermaid one by one,
knows their names and how they giggle,
with the deep red, rising sun,
and from the twilight on the waves,
above the deep and hidden caves,
she calls their names and listens long,
just as the slowly fading sun,
it disappears, the day now done.

And with the twilight on the waves,
these tiny maidens of the sea,
these sea maids, faces bright with glee,
their movements sleek and ever free,
they swim past reefs and sunken caves,
through twinkling twilight on the waves.

They swim to meet her gentle voice,
and swimming even, one by one,
and from her silver conch she hands them,
glowing earrings like the sun.

These golden earrings now adorn
these little mermaids' tiny ears,
below the foam and tides so steep,
while resting low in waters deep,
and worn above the reefs and caves,
and when the twilight's on the waves.

The Mermaid *Blossom* and the Lonesome Lotus Flower

Her fins soft pink like lotus petals,
pink as flamingos dancing free,
sweet *Blossom* glides along the waves
where flowers grow near colored caves,
and seeks a place along the shore
where lilies red as deep, dark wine
grow neat above the ocean floor
in silken spider web design.

Dark red flowers, neatly paired,
comingle with bright flowers, pink,
just like her fins, and like her hair,
along the shore in waters shared.

Flowers, pink, and deepest red,
they float among the cattails, tall,
among the starfish large and small,
below a silver waterfall.

It is there in flowing waters,
brown-red pelicans, they do call,
and in the mid-morn rising sun,
and on the water's surface, gleaming,
these flowers sparkle, all but one.

So, to this single, lonesome flower
Blossom swims with careful strokes,
and nestles close and listens softly,
to the bullfrogs' gentle croaks.

And soon this pink-white, lonesome flower,
it does adorn her flowing hair,
long and braided, painted pink,
and neat with beauty and with flair.

And so this sea maid's flowing hair,
unraveled rich in deep, pink bundles,
it glows and glistens like the sun does,
as *Blossom* swims back to the waves,
above the hidden, colored caves.

The Mermaid *Blissful* and the
Calm Before the Storms

The mermaid *Blissful*, ever wary,
of tempests raging out of sight,
she scans the yet calm, soothing waters
throughout the day into the night.

These placid waters, cool, serene,
painted blue with shades of green,
they whisper to her gentle touch,
as her hands do glide in rhythm,
flush across the colored prism
of their gently flowing waves
above the dark and hidden caves.

These gently, flowing waters whisper
in *Blissful's* ever patient ear.
They warn her of the dangers present
from darkened storms that rage so near.

So, to the placid, blue-green waves,
she sings her lovely maiden song,
and summons schools of red drum fish
to guide her through the raging storms.

She swims in circles 'round the ships,
with red drum fish along her side.
The sailors heed her mermaid chant.
It soothes. It calms. It does enchant,
and in the wind their sails unfurl,
as moonlight glows on *Blissful's* curls,
just as she leads them through the rain,
and through the lightening and the sleet,
and from the darkness of the storms
to peaceful waters they soon meet.

The Mermaid *Callula* and the
Night of the Colored Moon

When moonbeams float from starless skies,
when twilight lingers less,
above the waves where sea meets sky,
a colored moon does rest.

It is there *Callula* swims,
and sings her calming sea maid song.
It is there that dolphin fish,
as green as any emerald, bright,
they gather, glow, and linger long,
into the deepness of the night.

This colored moon does cast its glow
across the waves and calming waters.
These dolphin fish, their fins aglow,

like candles sparkling on an altar,
into the moonbeams they do dance,
across these placid ocean waves,
as sweet *Callula* glides in rhythm
with the moonbeams as they fade.

Soon the little mermaids gather,
along the rushes and the reeds,
as sweet *Callula*, with her moonbeams,
dancing off her colored beads,
colored like the moon above her,
deep blue-green and sparkling bright,
are cast into the shallow waters,
where little mermaids swim to catch them,
and wear them neat throughout the night.

The Mermaid *Symphony* and the Music from the Deep

When music from the hollow depths
bubbles from the waters deep,
when angelfish, as bright as gold,
leave their safe and favorite reef,
when starfish float upon the waves,
when treefish swim in swirls,
their golden fins striped deep, dark brown,
like *Symphony's* thick, auburn curls,
when harbor seals wake from their sleep,
and neon fish abound,
seahorses with a silver tint
are surely to be found.

It is there sweet *Symphony*,
her mermaid colors bright,

glows and glistens like a lantern
in the deep, dark, violet night.

She sings her lovely mermaid song,
to match the music from the depths,
as creatures from the cold, dark deep,
her lovely voice they surely seek,
do marvel at her maiden song,
and swim in circles ever long.

These creatures from the silent depths,
awakened from their midnight sleep,
her lovely music they do keep,
in hearts of gold through ages old,
throughout the depths deep, dark, and cold.

The Mermaid *Carmina* and the Golden Necklace

Around her lovely, maiden neck
a necklace does adorn,
and sparkles in the deep, dark night,
whenever it is worn.

And each night when the moon is full,
this necklace made of gold,
around her neck does glow and glisten,
as she recalls a legend, old.

This legend tells of sailors lost,
these sailors from the seven seas,
but only one who knows her name

will return, her love to claim,
and while she wears his necklace, gold,
throughout the oceans deep and cold.

As sweet *Carmina* softly listens
for the sounds of ship and crew,
and for her sailor love's sweet whispers,
in the night chants through and true,
this sparkling necklace glows and glistens,
into the darkness of the night,
as sweet *Carmina* waits and listens,
prays for his ship, a wondrous sight.

The Mermaid *Dulcetta* and the Ship Without a Sail

Dulcetta, with her scarlet fins,
that sparkle like a new-cut rose,
she waits and listens near the beach,
where starfish sleep in perfect rows,
where scarlet lilies, they do grow,
where blue-green waterfalls do flow.

These starfish, scarlet like her fins,
awaken to her mermaid song.
The sun a new day, it does bring,
just as her whispers linger long.

So, with these starfish at her side,
Dulcetta searches far and wide,
across the waters and the waves,
above the cold and hidden caves,
and for a ship without a sail,
a ship that only she has known,
a clipper ship lost in a storm,
her sailor lover all alone.

Each day she waits among the lilies,
scarlet like her glistening fins,
and among the starfish, bright,
that guide her through the deep, dark night.

She waits and listens, hoping for,
her sailor lover's gentle call,
far from his crow's nest high above
the rolling waves and ocean floor,
a gentle plea to hear once more.

His ship, alone, she prays to see,
gliding on an open sea,
a lonesome, solitary ship,
a clipper ship without a sail,
and so she waits through sleet and rain,
through thunder, dark, and pelting hail.

The Mermaid *Hopeful* and the Misting of the Moon

Her mermaid sisters do abound
when *Hopeful* is nearby
because the misting of the moon
is looming low and ever nigh.

As bright as any sunsets past,
her eyes do sparkle in the night,
and in the misting of the moon,
they sparkle like a diamond, bright.

And in this foggy, misty realm,
his clipper ship was lost from sight,
and so she waits as dewdrops drip,
her lovely finger on her lip,
and from the misty, golden air,
upon her long and flowing hair,
these lonely dewdrops do alight,
throughout the misting in the night.

Her sister mermaids know this legend
of how her sailor's ship was lost.
Its sails were tattered, torn, and ripped,
and covered deep in thick, white frost.

So, in the misting of the moon,
Hopeful and her sisters wait,
and praying from the deep, cold mist,

her sailor, lost, will blow a kiss,
and from his crow's nest ever high,
into the misting of the moon,
into her heart as tears are shed,
across this silent, calm lagoon.

Hopeful waits and prays he will
blow a sweet and gentle kiss,
as her heart is filled with bliss,
his kiss her one and only wish.

Across the sky the moon does dance,
with twinkling stars that seek romance,
and swimming close by, angelfish,
their golden tails, they do swish,
as *Hopeful's* lonely heart does swoon,
throughout the misting of the moon.

Their tails are golden like the air,
like *Hopeful's* golden, flowing hair.
These angelfish that swim in swirls,
they glow like *Hopeful's* golden curls,
and as she sings her maiden tune,
and as the stars seek out the moon,
her sister sirens, they do swoon,
throughout the misting of the moon.

The Mermaid *Moonbeam* and the
Moon with the Silver Flakes

Moonbeam has bright silver hair,
quite long and flowing in the breeze.
It dances in the silver moonlight,
as flakes of silver kiss the trees.

These ancient trees with rainbowed leaves,
reach out to moonbeams high above,
across these calm and quiet waters,
across this green lagoon, so deep,
and like a pure, white swan in love,
they capture moonbeams white as doves,
as ancient starfish, they do sleep
below the waves in caverns deep.

It is here that *Moonbeam* waits,
while singing out her maiden song,
throughout the flaking of the moon,
across this deep and calm lagoon,
a sweet and lovely, gentle tune.

So, to her calming tune they come,
silver koi fish one by one.
They swim in neat and perfect swirls,
their fins as silver as her curls.

They listen to her maiden song,
their circles perfect, neat, and strong.
Into the moonbeam path they swim,
and in the waters, they do skim.

The line they swim is tight and straight,
and toward a solitary form,
and quaking in the moonbeam path,
a lonesome form in shadows cast.

So, in the twinkling, moonbeam light,
throughout the gloaming in the night,
and as these silver flakes do dance,
as lovely *Moonbeam* seeks romance,
around the silver shadows cast,
a rowboat from a distant shore,
seeks out her presence evermore.

With silver koi fish by her side,
to this rowboat *Moonbeam* glides,
and on the shoreline flush with weeds,
among the rushes and the reeds,
with cattails swishing in the breeze,
this long-lost sailor steps ashore,
his eyes as sparkling as before.

The Mermaid *Icey Blue* and the Penguins on the Ice

In deep, dark waters, icy cold,
huddled thick on sheets of ice,
small penguins wait for *Icey Blue*,
to guide them through the deep, dark night.

On her breath frost lingers still,
as she swims in ice-filled waters,
toward the ice sheet where they wait,
praying, hoping, she's not late.

Soon these anxious, little penguins,
and stranded in the waters, cold,
are placed upon the hunched-up backs
of gray-white whales, eyes of old,

while legends of the seven seas,
in their hearts, they do unfold.

Icey Blue has deep blue fins,
as blue as any ocean deep,
and from the ice shelf she does swim,
with whales woke from their midnight sleep.

Her mermaid chanting, loud and strong,
leads these whales, some black as coal,
as orcas swim in thick, dark shoals,
and guide them to an island, near,
to blue-green waters calm and clear,
away from danger and from fear.

26

The Mermaid *Jasmina* and the Little Lost Whale

Jasmina is an easy swimmer.
Eyes on fire, they do glimmer,
in the darkness of the evening,
as she searches far and wide,
in the frothy, gray-white tide,
and for a lonely, little whale,
lost among thick, pelting hail,
lost in sleet and pounding thunder,
and in a tempest raging under
skies as dark as midnight shadows,
in the deepness and the shallows.

She sings her mermaid melody,
loud and clear throughout the storm,
and hoping, wishing, it is heard,
throughout the sea, as it is stirred,
by driving rain and icy sleet,
and hoping their sweet voices meet.

In the din of rain and thunder,
a tiny voice calls from the deep.

Jasmina swims in steady strokes
to where their voices, they soon meet.

And there a small, gray, lonely whale,
and huddled in dark shadows, thick,
and lost in waters cold and deep,
below the waves deep, dark, and steep,
does hurry, oh, so, ever quick,
to hear her lovely maiden song,
his swimming fast and ever long.

He nestles close along her side,
among the foaming, rolling tides,
among the seaweed, floating, thick,
as sweet *Jasmina,* she does swim.
Her strokes are measured, even, trim.

Above these cold and frigid waters,
this small, gray whale close by her side,
and with the surface, ever gleaming,
to the mainland, they do glide.

28

The Mermaid *Ariana* and the Silver Earrings

Silver earrings lost at sea,
are hidden deep below a reef,
a reef as bright as sparkling silver,
a reef where copper rockfish dwell,
or so the ancient legend tells.

And *Ariana* knows this legend,
and where these copper rockfish sleep,
below a reef as bright as silver,
along a beach and silver river,
a river dark and ever deep,
and where these earrings, it is told,
were worn by mermaid queens of old.

She whistles to the copper rockfish,
their scales aglow in orange and gold,
their eyes as sharp and darkly ancient,
as the seven seas are old.

They guide her to a passage, narrow,
below this dazzling, silver reef,
and there a chest lies in the shadows,
a treasure chest beyond belief.

But *Ariana* only seeks
lost earrings, silver, like the waves,
when moonlight dances over them,
above the deep, forbidden caves.

These earrings once were worn by queens,
sweet sirens of the seven seas.
Mermaid queens, and one her mother,
they sparkle like none of the other
gems that fill this treasure chest,
where silver curls are gently pressed,
as she clutches close these earrings
and from this chest below this reef,
she signals to her friends, the rockfish,
that her journey is complete.

The Mermaid *Lucetta* and the Parrotfish

Lucetta has bright, golden eyes,
as bright as any shining sun,
and in the shadows of the twilight,
her hair does mimic silken moonlight,
a spider's web so softly spun.

Parrotfish with rainbow fins,
and scales that glow with colors, bright,
they guide *Lucetta* through the twilight,
among vermillion rockfish swimming,
in the looming, yellow light.

They lead her to a quiet place,
to where a sunken ship does rest,
to where a sunken treasure chest
is filled with silver and with gold,
beneath the waters clear but cold.

Jeweled top snails, they do rest
upon this treasure chest of old.
Their perfect patterns colored neat,
and painted thick in dazzling gold,
glow and glisten, glimmer, bright,
into the darkness of the night.

It is there *Lucetta* sings
her maiden song, sublime and sweet.
It is then these jeweled top snails,
listen softly, careful, neat,
and then unlock this chest of gold,
and swim to waters clear but cold.

So, to this chest *Lucetta* swims,
and finds this ancient, mermaid locket,
gold and silver, lined with sapphires,
then to the surface like a rocket,
she swims to moonlight on the waves,
above the dark and secret caves.

The Mermaid *Astral* and the Night of a Thousand Stars

The mermaid *Astral* swims at night,
beginning in the dim twilight.
Her deep, dark fins are hard to see,
underneath the purple sea,
but her silver eyes do sparkle
like the stars above her glowing,
soft and twinkling in the heavens,
like her silver hair that's flowing,
down along her slender shoulders,
starlight, bright, above her growing,
and leading her to warmer waters,
her eyes like shining silver dollars,
a thousand stars above her, bright,
and dancing in the deep, dark night.

It is there that silver marlins,
they swim in circles ever tight,
and as the waters slowly darken,
their sparkling colors lost from sight,
in the churning, swirling waters,
in the deep, dark, velvet night,
Astral waits to follow them,
to guide her with their colors, bright.

And it is there throughout the night,
the heavens glow with starlight, bright,
just as these dancing, silver marlins,
they dance in rhythm out of sight,
and under waves where *Astral* waits,
for their steepness and their rocking
to slowly cease and to abate,

these sparkling, silver-coated marlins,
point to a shining, silver gate.

Then to this sparkling gate she swims,
sweet *Astral* with her mermaid chant,
and while these dazzling, silver marlins,
they do listen. They do dance,
above the seaweed thick in bunches,
along a beach with reeds and rushes,
below the moonlight ever flashing,
and as the purple waves come crashing.

It is there in waters deep,
below the crashing, purple waves,
near secret, rainbow-colored caves,
these silver marlins know the way,
and with their silver tails swishing,
they open up a silver gate,
as *Astral*, eyes aglow, does wait.

And there she finds a treasure lost,
a whaling ship lost in a storm,
inside of which she finds a chest,
with silver coins and silver crests.

With silver marlins as her guide,
throughout the purple waves she glides,
her mermaid pouch fixed to her waist,
and filled with silver coins and crests,
these crests of silver soon to rest,
in mermaids' hair so neatly pressed.

The Mermaid *Zarina* and the Emerald Harp

A yellow rockfish at her side,
Zarina, swimming, she does glide
above the waters, sapphire blue,
and under skies, a purple hue.

Above the waves, an island view
does linger on the far-off shore,
a place the rockfish lead her to,
a place that she has seen before.

And at this secret, hidden place,
where yellow rockfish swim in shoals,
it is there the legend tells,
and near this island neat with palms,
and under skies as calm as psalms,
an emerald harp is hidden deep,
and in a cave, along a reef.

A yellow rockfish at her side,
its tail as bright as shining gold,
along this reef it swims in circles,
a colored reef of blues and purples.

And there *Zarina*, she does dive,
to find inside this purple cave,
below the calm and placid waters,
an emerald harp as it is played.

Zarina sings her maiden song.
It floats into this colored cave
where music from a harp does sound,
sweet and clear and lasting long,
such lovely music, like her song.

Into this purple cave she swims,
a yellow rockfish as her guide,
and there an octopus, deep green,
her eyes like emeralds of a queen,
plays on her harp a melody,
so soft and calming, and serene.

Zarina waits and listens low,
as the music from the deep,
ignites a passion in her eyes,
her ruby lips cannot disguise.

This passion deep and lasting long,
it urges her to swim away,
and leave this octopus, so green,
her lovely music, sweet, serene,
floating, swirling, there to stay,
throughout the silence of the night,
to calm and soothe throughout the day,
the lonely creatures of the deep,
below the waves cold, dark, and steep.

36

The Mermaid *Angelina* and the Angelfish

The angelfish, they know the way
to where a sailor lost at sea
was floating through the night and day
in seaweed, thick, and tumbling waves,
above the caverns and the caves,
in waters near a scarlet reef,
where angelfish, they swim and play.

King angelfish, their tails so bright,
and golden like the mid-day sun,
lead *Angelina* to this reef,
her heartfelt duty almost done.

These angelfish, deep blue their scales,
as blue as lazy, silent skies,
and shaded blue, like skins of whales,
hazy blue, their pinpoint eyes.

These angelfish, they glow and glisten.
Their merriment, they can't disguise.
Their eyes that sparkle in the moonlight
shine bright like *Angelina's* eyes,
as she dives and listens low,
for the sailor's silent pleas,

praying he is still among,
the floating seaweed in the sea.

And soon she finds him softly breathing,
and clutching to a wooden plank.
She whistles to the angelfish,
and to the depths deep, dark, and dank,
they swim to summon blue-green whales,
as vibrant as their sparkling scales.

And soon upon these whales' backs,
behemoths of the seven seas,
lost in the waves the silent pleas
of a long-lost sailor, found,
as *Angelina* and this sailor,
to the mainland they do glide,
the angelfish in shoals and shoals,
swimming smoothly by their side.

Across the blue-green waves they glide,
and to the shoreline they do ride,
this sailor, found, and *Angelina,*
and to an island neat with palms,
among clear waters cool and calm.

The Mermaid *Luciana* and the Deep Velvet Lilies

Lilies deep and lasting long,
under coral, turquoise blue,
above the soft and pleasant song,
sweet *Luciana* sings so true,
they glow and glisten, as they listen,
while sparkling with a velvet hue.

Legends tell these lilies, deep,
mark the spot where zebrafish,
their scales striped deeply blue and white,
they swim in shoals throughout the night,
and guard a cavern deep and wide,
where buried treasure lies inside.

So, to these lilies she does glide,
these zebrafish close by her side,
and singing out her maiden song,
her hair is scarlet, thick, and long.

Her eyes like rubies, red and deep,
and flowing, tumbling hair to match,
she spies a treasure chest and latch,
and made of gold with silver pins,
a treasure from the deep within.

These zebrafish swim to her side,
and in this cavern once inside,
this treasure chest with silver pins,
an orphan of the seven seas,
is opened wide with silver keys,
found on top this chest of old,
inside a treasure deep with gold.

But *Luciana* seeks not gold,
she only seeks a silver cross,
a sailor's cross, quite neat, and bright,
that she will wear forever more,
throughout the day into the night.

This sailor's cross was lost at sea,
or so the fabled legend tells,
a sailor of the seven seas,
his ship complete with copper bells,
that rang and rung in harmony,
when mermaid queens of old,
swam to his ship to welcome him,
in waters clear but cold.

The Mermaid *Sunshine* and the Maiden with the Golden Slippers

An island rests alone among
deep, silent waters green and blue,
and crystal-clear like starless skies,
that rain and thunder can't disguise.

So, to this island *Sunshine* swims
to meet a sweet and tiny maiden,
the daughter of a sailor lost.
His ship was empty and unladen
when a tempest wrought its fury
in the deep, dark, desperate night.
His crew and ship were never found,
lost in the storm and lost from sight.

So, to this island *Sunshine* swims.
A tiny maiden, hair of gold,
eyes like sunsets, waits to meet her,
under skies deep, dark, and cold.

Upon her feet, bright, golden slippers,
as moonlight in her eyes does flicker,
and in her hand a ring of old,
and made of Spanish, sparkling gold,
she waits in golden, slippered feet,
the mermaid *Sunshine* soon to meet.

When *Sunshine* swims along the shore,
the skies are deep and dark no more.
The coldness gone, the sunshine bright,
as slippered feet come into sight.

So, from her outstretched hand a ring,
as golden as sweet *Sunshine's* hair,
is handed to this mermaid fair,
and from a maiden from the mainland,
and to a maiden of the sea,
and once worn by her sailor love,
in seas of dread with tempests thick.
It now rests on her hand as she,
returns to waves where she should be.

The Mermaid *Madrigal* and the Silver Waterfall

At a place where swans do swim,
bright silver are their sparkling colors.
A place where silver rivers flow,
it is a place devoid of snow,
as sundrops on the lilies glisten,
and silver-streaked in shining sun,
a place where silver cattails grow,
a place where silver beaches glow.

Madrigal, her hair bright silver,
as silver as the waterfall,
where silver lilies grow in bunches,
neat among the cattails, tall,
she reaches out to touch the waters,
as the waterfall does flow,
into a river bright as silver,
and where the silver lilies grow.

These waters soothe. They hypnotize,
bring tears to quiet, silver eyes,
as she recalls the legend, old,
about a sailor brave and bold,
whose ship was lost in midnight storms,
surrounded by deep waves in swarms,
and lost among the silver lilies,
that float among the silver swans,
his ship's bell colored deeply bronze,
that washed upon the silver shore,
the only clue to where his ship,
could be found for evermore.

So, as she swims among the silver
swans that glide across the river,
and silver as the waterfall,
she dives in deep and secret waters.
The ship's bronze bell, alone, it calls.

And in the depths she finds this bell,
copper, bronze, and tarnished dull,
and ringing with a solemn knell,
and by a squid as bright as moonlight,
exactly as the legend tells,
a silver squid that rings this bell.

And to this squid she sings her song,
a lovely mermaid melody,
and from the bell this squid removes
a single, solitary key.

And so this squid in whispers, low,
sings out the place where rests a chest,
and where her shining, silver locket,
and once worn as a sailor's crest,
around his neck in crows' nests, high,
will be found in waters, deep,
surrounded by a silver sky.

This key she holds, then finds this chest,
just as the silver squid did tell,
and in it rests a locket, gold.
Her picture neatly does unfold,
as it is opened, breath held tight,
as *Madrigal* with easy strokes,
swims with silver eyes so bright,
and underneath a silver moon,
into the twinkling, silver night.

So, with this locket, once a gift,
a sea nymph to a sailor love,
and as her maiden song was sung,
and on a beach white as a dove,
before he sailed the seven seas,
in deep, dark storms, and gentle breeze,
she swims to moonbeams on the water,
just like the octopus had taught her.

The Mermaid *Tianna* and the Castle Under the Sea

Looming in the twilight thunder,
looming low in seas of dread,
a castle deep, dark, and deserted,
calls out to her with words unsaid.

Tianna dives in gray-green waters,
churning in the open sea,
and to the sounds of sea kraits singing,
their yellow lips as bright as gold,
Tianna follows close the ringing,
coming from this castle, old.

These sea kraits swim in even lines,
and guide her to the ringing bell,
inside a castle dark as thunder,
just as the mermaid legend tells.

Into the hollow, gloomy waters,
into the silence of the sea,
these sea kraits with their duty done,
and with their shining, golden smiles,
into the darkness they do flee,
into the green-gray, lonely sea,
to surf and waves, and frothing foam,
and to a place they call their home.

The castle's gate is opened wide,
sweet ringing from the bell inside,
sea kraits no longer by her side.

Sweet music from this ringing bell,
leads *Tianna*, swimming slowly,
to the sounds, serene, and holy.

Then in a room with candles, bright,
and looming in the candlelight,

a figure of a sailor, lost,
does ring this bell, so sweet and low.
His shadowed form, it seems to glow,
like lanterns in the deep, dark night,
like swans, their colors pure and white.

He beckons her to swim inside.
This sailor, lost, his form does float
just like a specter in the air,
just like *Tianna*'s golden hair,
and dancing neat and ever slow,
and dancing in the candle's glow.

And to this form in steady strokes,
she swims inside this castle, old,
and from his palm this ghost-like sailor,
he hands to her a key of gold.

Then *Tianna*, eyes on fire,
as red as sunsets on a beach,
she grasps this key and holds it tight,
just as the ghost-like sailor form,
it disappears into the light.

And from the candlelight still streaming,
and with her golden eyes still gleaming,
Tianna, with this golden key,
she swims to moonlight, ever beaming,
above this calm and gentle sea.

And of the octopus-told legends
of where this golden key will fit,
it soon will rest with mermaid queens,
who know the legends through and true,
about the seven seas so blue,
and what this golden key can do.

The Mermaid Queens, Three, and the Golden Key

Around a moss-covered rock they sat,
three mermaid queens and an old sea cat.
Tianna, the mermaid, her smile sparkling silver,
it glowed and it glimmered like a slow-moving river.

A key as golden as her free-flowing hair,
was handed politely with caution and care,
to the first siren queen, her fins green as the sea,
as *Tianna* smiled softly at the mermaid queens,
three.

The old sea cat sitting quite in-between,
her eyes like emeralds with a deep forest sheen,
moved ever so close to the queen and the key,
a locket on her neck dangling fancy and free.

She purred like a sea cat on midnight watch,
as sweet siren songs flowed from conch after
conch,
'round an old whaling ship where a sailor above,
listened for chants from his young mermaid love.

And now this gold key in mermaid queen hands,
was placed in the locket from seafaring lands.
The old sea cat's eyes, they glowed and they
glimmered.
The mermaid queens' eyes were dark green as
they shimmered.

The purring of the cat was lost in the breeze,
as teardrops flowed from the mermaid queens,
three.
From the locket a stone, a bright topaz crystal,
brought smiles to their faces, fancy and blissful.

And now this bright topaz, as blue as the oceans,
as round and as perfect as a blue moon at night,
sparkling and glowing like an old wizard's potion,
and shining like night fires, dancing ever so bright,
was placed quite securely with caution and care,
into a crown made of gold that mermaid queens
wear.

These mermaid queens, three,
all smiled with delight,
as this crown of the oceans
danced in the moonlight.

It was placed on the head of a maiden quite fair.
It fit rather snugly over sparkling, gold hair,
and now there were four, mermaid queens of
the sea,
as an old sea cat purred in the soft midnight
breeze.

The Mermaid *Abba* and the Silver Squids

Under reefs where sea squirts sleep,
under waves deep, dark, and steep,
silver squids, they glow and glisten,
and swim in swirls, as *Abba* listens.

And from the silver harps they play,
sweet music echoes from the depths.
Sweet *Abba* listens to this music
from where these silver squids do rest.

But *Abba*, in her heart of hearts,
seeks only one, a silver harp,
a harp that glows with sapphires, bright,
that she will carry with her always
throughout the misting in the night.

This silver harp with sapphires, bright,
the ancient mermaid legend tells,
was made for mermaid queens of old,
and lost in waves deep, dark, and cold.

So, as this lovely music blossoms,
from the surface *Abba* dives,
to find this silver harp so rare.
She dives with caution and with care.

So, as these silver squids do whisper,
in these hollow, lonely depths,
she hears her lovely, mermaid name,
her eyes now flashing and aflame.
Sweet sounds of *Abba* beckon her,
this silver harp for her to claim.

The Mermaid *Agraciana* and the Starfish on the Beach

Agraciana knows the way
to where an ivory beach does glow,
below the moonlight and the moonbeams,
along a reef where cattails grow,
and where a silent river flows.

It is there that starfish linger,
their colors deep blue, red, and gold,
and that is where the treasure lies,
or so the mermaid legend goes.

Agraciana knows this legend,
knows where the colored starfish sleep,
upon an ivory beach with cattails,
beside the water cold and deep.

It is there she swims in moonlight,
a starfish of the brightest gold,
her guide to sunken, hidden treasure,
its eyes as ancient and as old,
as the seven seas are cold.

But it is here in warmer waters,
and where these colored starfish sleep,
and where *Agraciana* dives,
below a rainbow-colored reef,
and where an ancient crown does rest,
a crown of mermaid queens of old,
a crown of silver and of gold.

The Mermaid *Crystal* and the Silver Swans

In waters still and clear as glass,
a mermaid bright as crystal swims.
Her hair is braided, long, and sleek.
A reddish glow adorns each cheek.

She swims among the silver swans,
and from the palms float purple fronds,
upon these neat and placid waters,
along a beach where *Crystal* skims
across the slowly moving waves,
above the secret, hidden caves.

It is here that silver swans,
they swim in perfect symmetry,
and below their perfect circles,
deep in a blue-green placid sea,
lies a jeweled crown of old,
and lost by sailors brave and bold.

This jeweled crown once worn by queens,
mermaid queens with sparkling eyes,
was lost in seas deep, dark, and cold.
or so the legend, it is told.

The mermaid *Crystal*, she does dive,
underneath these swimming swans,
and below these purple fronds,

into a blue-green silent sea,
to find this jeweled crown of old,
that's trimmed with silver and with gold,
once worn by mermaid queens, renown,
or so the legend, it is told.

And on the bottom of a reef,
rainbowed thick in red and green,
she finds this ancient, jeweled crown,
and guarded there in depths unseen,
by damselfish, their colors brown,
their eyes deep, dark, like queens' renown,
and swimming circles, perfect, neat,
around this shining, jeweled crown,
and so their eyes, they soon do meet.

Then to the surface they did swim,
and then across the waves they skimmed,
these damselfish, their eyes aglow,
the legend left deep, down below.

Into the twilight they did go,
swimming neat and ever slow,
and as the twilight it did grow,
and as this jeweled crown did glow,
this legend old from long ago,
was left in seas deep, down below.

54

The Mermaid *Coralina* and the Cave of Wonders

Near a cave no sailor's seen,
under waves deep emerald-green,
lies a reef where starfish sleep,
beneath the surface cold and deep.

These starfish bright as golden suns,
they guard the entrance to this cave,
and listen for a mermaid's song,
sweet and low and lasting long.

Coralina, fins deep green,
green like emeralds in the cave,
gently sings her maiden song,
as these starfish swim in swirls,
her eyes as bright as shining pearls.

These starfish watching ever close,
hear *Coralina's* gentle song,
and swirl in rhythm to the sounds,
of her voice that lingers long.

Into this cave she swims in tandem,
with the movements of these starfish,
their swirling circles neat, not random,
as *Coralina* seeks the ransom
from pirate ships and treasure chests,
of gold doubloons and moon-like crests,
and soon to rest 'round princess' necks.

The Mermaid *Xema* and the Purple Stingrays

Xema's hair is thick with curls.
Her eyes are bright as yellow pearls.
Her fins are purple like her hair,
and like the stingrays she does seek,
below the waves cold, dark, and steep,
are hard to see in waters deep.

These purple stingrays swim in pairs,
along a purple-colored reef.
They dance in rhythm to the moonlight,
in the sparkling night so brief,
inviting her to follow closely,
until their eyes do slowly meet,
and to the moonbeams on the water,
she swims in rhythm with the stingrays,
just like the octopus had taught her.

These purple stingrays know the way
to where a sunken ship does rest.
They swim in swirls in silky foam,
above their silent, hidden home,
'cause that is where this ship does rest,
and that is where an old sea chest
waits among the sea snakes, deep,
below the swirling waves so steep,
with hidden treasure, it does keep.

The mermaid legend *Xema* knows,
about this treasure chest so deep,
in her beating heart she keeps,
as these purple stingrays lead her,
to where the ancient sea snakes sleep.

But it is not a chest of silver,
nor a chest of shining gold,
sweet *Xema* seeks in waters cold.
She seeks a trident, ringed with rubies,
that glows like orange-red burning fires,
embedded in the ocean bottom,
among deep red and black sea spiders.

So, following these purple stingrays,
their tails like comets, glowing, streaming,
Xema's eyes are flashing, gleaming,
across the twilight's purple mist.
Her purple fins, the waves do kiss.

So, in these deep, forbidden waters,
and in the silence of the sea,
in her heart sweet *Xema* keeps
these mermaid legends as she seeks
where these dark sea snakes, they sleep.

But when awakened they do hiss,
but lovely *Xema's* gentle kiss,
urges them to leave this place,
and swim away to waters, cold,
as *Xema's* song from mermaids, old,
does float across this silent sea,
as she grasps the trident tightly,
and to the stingrays blows a kiss,
just as their purple tails do swish.

58

The Pirate, the Painted Parrots, and the Sea Nymph *Poema*

On large, bent shoulders stiff and square,
and under braided pirates' hair,
two parrots with their colors, bright,
they caw and caw into the night.

This pirate with deep, coal-black eyes,
a limp his peg leg can't disguise,
he strolls the deck in sunlight, bright,
into the fleeting evening's light.

Sweet *Poema,* a sea nymph fair,
with sparkling, wavy, auburn hair,
she swims in circles 'round his ship,
her dainty fingers on her lips,
calls to these parrots, one by one.
Her curls dance in the midday sun.

This pirate with a dark red patch,
on one eye just like a latch,
a twisted hat, gray-black and worn,
and blood-red trousers, ripped and torn,
an earring dangling from his ear,
across his face a pirate's sneer,
a voice that cracks and loudly shook,
and for one hand a golden hook,
he listens close to hear her song,
his pacing quick and ever long,
across the polished, shiny deck,
a red bandana 'round his neck.

These parrots caw, then fly away
to where *Poema* swims alone,
and on a rock along the shore,
they land and perch and caw some more.

The legend sweet *Poema* knows,
about these birds that fly together,
through sleet and rain and pounding thunder,
in winters, deep, and summer weather,
these painted parrots, red and green,
with streaks of yellow in between,
will lead her to a sea ledge, where
a rock shaped like a captain's chair,
rests near a chest in deep, dark sand,
and so she stretches out her hand,
and urges them to lead the way,
to find this treasure where it lay.

This pirate with his hardened face,
and with his sleeves that end in lace,
his knee-high boots thick, dark, and black,
his nose just like an old smokestack,
on his pirate ship does stay,
his face a darkened, charcoal gray,
a skull-and-crossbones waving free,
above a blue-gray, rolling sea,
a pirate on the open sea,
and with one eye, he squints to see,
to where these painted parrots fly,
a gleam in sweet *Poema's* eyes.

The Mermaid *Briella* and the Golden Sand Dollars

Sand dollars, gold, and bright as moonlight,
glimmer in the twilight, streaming,
below a waterfall where moonbeams
dance across the waters, gleaming.

It is a place *Briella* knows
a place devoid of sleet and snow,
of thunder, dark, and driving rain,
of hail and squalls, and tempests blaring.
It is a place of love and caring,
a place where just below the waves,
sand dollars, golden like the sun,
sleeping deep near hidden caves,
are waiting for her gentle song,
to wake them from their slumber, long.

So, in these caves, but only one,
moonlight glows, but not the sun.
It is where sea urchins sparkle,
their golden colors dancing, gleaming,
across the waves with moonbeams streaming,
and sparkling in the midnight air,
and sparkling like *Briella's* hair,

and braided thick in golden bundles,
and flowing deep along her shoulders,
and like the octopus had told her,
Briella's hair, like golden moonlight,
will lead her to the place she seeks,
a place below a colored reef,
and where sand dollars, they do sleep.

And in the dancing midnight air,
they slumber near a treasure chest,
in waters, cold, and buried deep.
They slumber in their midnight sleep.

This treasure chest of legends told,
holds jewels and gems and crowns of old.
Upon its lid sand dollars sleep,
and when they hear *Briella's* song,
they waken from their midnight sleep,
then swim away to waters, deep.

Briella, now, this chest does open,
hidden treasure, hers to keep,
and so she swims to silent moonlight,
as the starfish, they do sleep.

The Mermaid *Charissa* and the Swirling Treefish

Swirling treefish, striped deep green,
with lips as red as rubies, bright,
they swim in placid, patient waters,
and under twinkling, soft moonlight.

So, as *Charissa*'s maiden song,
echoes through the silent night,
and past the rushes and the reeds,
and through sad, swaying willow trees,
the stars, above, align in magic,
above this lovely, sandy beach,
where cattails to the stars do reach.

It is here sea otters play,
in the sunlight through the day,
but in the night they soundly sleep,
as do most creatures of the deep.

But in the morning burning, bright,
the golden sun appears again.
It is then that harbor seals
emerge in pairs from out their dens,
to greet these treefish as they swirl,
and as the blue-gray waters curl,
around this cave where treasure rests,
and buried deep next to a nest
where spiders of the deep do sleep,
and in their webs blue pearls they keep.

And so these treefish know the way,
as sweet *Charissa* sings her song,

the otters and the seals now gone,
Charissa's hair deep, dark, and long,
and flowing down along her shoulders
as she swims like silent moonlight,
just like the octopus had shown her.

With treefish swimming at her side,
below the flowing, yellow tide,
the mermaid legend beckons her,
to find this place from long ago
in waters dancing deep below.

The spiders, only, all alone,
they hear her lovely maiden song,
and dance in rhythm with her tone,
a lovely siren melody,
born of the ancient tides and waves,
resounding through dark, hidden caves,
and on their webs as fine as silk,
and guarded by black spiders, three,
are held blue pearls bright as the sea.

So, to their web *Charissa* swims,
along with treefish swimming, free,
to pluck these pearls as blue as oceans,
these pearls as blue as wizards' potions,
and made for maidens of the sea,
and made for sea nymphs swimming free,
and then to swim to sunsets past,
and to a place where she should be.

The Mermaid *Cosima* and the Trident in the Moonlight

A jeweled scepter, legends tell,
adorned with sparkling, sapphire rings,
that once were worn by mermaid queens,
the brides of ancient mariner kings,
is buried deep in sandy waters,
and under moonlight, in between,
rocks as ancient as the sea,
and guarded by large sea snakes, three.

These sea snakes, three, are different colors,
bright red, bright green, and topaz blue.
They guard this scepter day and night,
through storms and squalls and tempests raging,
and waiting for a mermaid's song,
their colors deep but never changing.

And when this maiden melody,
this siren song from ages past,
into the depths, as it is cast,
does float below the silent waves,
these serpents of the seven seas,
swim off to deep, dark, hidden caves.

They hear *Cosima's* charming song,
and leave this precious jeweled wand,
just as *Cosima*, eyes aglow,
does claim this scepter, swims beyond
the deep, dark, waters, cold and still,
the mermaid legend now fulfilled.

The Mermaid *Duvessa* and the Darkest of Evenings

When harbor seals wake from their sleep,
and in their dens, their young they keep,
warm and safe and still asleep,
ascending from the waters deep,
jellyfish do swim in line,
just as their vibrant colors shine,
around a beach serene and calm,
as waves do kiss *Duvessa's* palms.

These jellyfish with lions' manes,
seek out *Duvessa's* gentle song,
and as her palms caress the waters,
her lovely chanting lingers long,
into the evening, dark as thunder,
as these jellyfish swim under,
a lonesome moon cast in the shadows
of deep, dark clouds, above the shallows.

It is there these jellyfish,
have waited 'til the sun has set,
their swimming perfect, neat, but yet,
they seek out moonlight on the waters,
throughout the darkness, out of sight,

their golden colors dancing, bright,
just like a beacon, glowing, flashing,
as the deep, dark, waves come crashing.

Duvessa, waiting, listens low,
these jellyfish, their movements slow,
then waking from her evening rest,
the evening dark as sea snakes' nests,
Duvessa dives in waters, gloomy,
and in this darkness on the waves,
deep below are cold, dark caves,
and that is where their manes will glow,
these jellyfish that swim quite slow.

They lead *Duvessa* to a place
where treasure rests from sunken ships,
and like a lighted candle, bright,
they guide her in the deep, dark night,
to find this secret, hidden treasure,
of bracelets, silver, combs of gold,
of strings of pearls and diamond rings,
assorted coins and other things,
then lead her to her mermaid home.

The Mermaid *Edra* and the Lost Island

An island in the sunlight, bright,
is guarded through the day and night
by shoals of fantailed-fish, deep orange,
as *Edra* swims with silent strokes,
the reefs deep green with vibrant cloaks
of cattails, thick, and rushes, tall.
She swims to where the fish do call.

These fantailed fish, *Calico* their name,
they swim in circles 'round the reef,
and *Edra*, to their gentle calls,
sings out her maiden song for all.

These fantailed fish, deep orange their fins,
and bright as any glowing sun,
they lead her to a rock shelf where
red lilies grow in fragrant air.

They swim in circles and in pairs,
these orange-red fish, their colors bright,
while *Edra* sings her siren song,
throughout the day into the night.

And at this rock shelf green with moss,
a solitary starfish rests.
Its colors scarlet like her hair,
it guards a hidden seabird's nest.

These seabirds all have flown away,
the nest deserted but not empty,
and in this nest from sunsets past,
glowing, gleaming, shining, tempting,
and on thatched twigs just like a throne,
does rest an ancient, scarlet stone.

Its colors vibrant and reflecting
Edra's hair in silent moonlight
and holy like nuns genuflecting,
its colors deep and glowing bright,
this gemstone of the ancient seas,
with colors dancing in the breeze,
and scarlet like the starfish, waiting,
throughout the deep, dark, velvet night,
glows in the shadows of the moonbeams,
its scarlet colors, glowing, streaming,
and all around white moon flakes beaming.

These dancing colors, shining, bright,
this gemstone, ancient as the seas,
to *Edra* is a wondrous sight,
was worn by mermaid queens of old,
around their necks, their crowns of gold,
and sparkled in their midnight slumber,
through winters, dark, and golden summers.

The Mermaid *Juliana* and the
Rainbows of a Thousand Colors

Rainbows of a thousand colors,
and glowing deeply in the night,
to *Juliana* they do beckon,
to *Juliana* they invite
her to swim in crystal waters,
and to their ends where treasure rests,
and to the spot where golden crowns
are hidden deep in old sea chests.

Around these wondrous, rainbow colors,
rainbow fish do swim in pairs,
in the swirling, curling waters,
in the sunset, looming, gloaming,
in the waves gray-white and foaming.

They lead her to a river streaming,
above a blue-green waterfall,
its waters colored like bright rainbows,
moonbeams on its surface gleaming,
cloaks of silver almost seeming
silver like her eyes now beaming.

For at this point where water glistens,
sweet *Juliana* slowly listens,
as the rock crabs, red as fire,
tap their claws as they advance,
and to this sea chest filled with gold,
just as the rainbow fish do dance.

Beneath this waterfall and river,
diving deep, she takes a chance,
and there along the sandy bottom,
rainbow colors now receding,
tapping from the rock crabs pleading,
sweet *Juliana,* close, does follow
these rainbow fish, their colors vibrant,
and swimming silently and leading,
and close nearby are sea snakes feeding,
and soon to *Juliana's* chanting,
they are listening. They are heeding,
and swim to waters deep and dark,
where they will nest and make their mark.

These rainbow fish and *Juliana,*
swimming past these sea snakes' nests,
now swim to where this treasure rests.
They swim in neat and perfect lines,
past reefs with sharp and spindly spines.

So, to this rusty, treasure chest,
and filled with silver coins and gold,
with *Juliana,* eyes aglow,
these rainbow fish and *Juliana,*
they do glide in waters, cold,
this mermaid legend, ancient, bold,
now fulfilled as it was told.

The Mermaid *Tamara* and The Mermaid Twins

The mermaid twins, one blue as topaz,
the other red as rubies, bright,
they swim together through the moonlight,
into the deep, dark, violet night.

These mermaid twins were born at midnight
and underneath a colored moon,
and in the gloaming of the evening,
and swimming through a still lagoon,
they now pursue a long, lost treasure,
just as the mermaid legend tells,
and buried deep below the waters,
just as the swirling sea does swell.

And under waterfalls that mist,
Tamara blows a gentle kiss,
just as these mermaid twins do swim
to hear her sweet and soothing song,
as moonbeams linger bright and long.

And underneath this dancing moonlight,
their sparkling colors glowing bright,
these mermaid twins swim ever slowly,
their movements neat, serene, and holy.

Then waiting there with swishing fins,
Tamara with her siren song,
calls slowly to the mermaid twins,
to follow her and swim along,
to dive for sunken treasure, deep,
below the purple waves so steep.

She blows a long and gentle kiss,
as the mermaid twins dive deep,
and underneath a colored moon,
to unknown waters dark and steep,
and in their hearts the mermaid legend,
fervently, they both do keep.

Tamara dives and follows slowly,
the mermaid twins, eyes glowing, holy,
soft and warm, like midnight slumber,
and seeking treasure lost in summer,
and when a clipper ship did sink,
in waters deep with coral, pink.

And there below the pounding surf
pink coral grows near colored caves,
but only one contains the treasure,
and under rolling, rocking waves.

So, in this cave of turquoise blue,
and swimming closely, just the two,
these mermaid twins, *Tamara* near,
this hidden treasure does appear.

So, with their mermaid pouches brimming,
with dazzling gemstones lost at sea,
these lovely mermaids, mermaids three,
to the surface, they do swim,
across the blue-gray waves they skim.

The Mermaid *Hypathia* and the Golden Seahorse

One is crimson, red as fire,
the other waterfall deep blue,
and to the treasures, they do lead,
waterfalls that number two.

But in the misting from these falls,
and underneath these waterfalls,
a golden seahorse waits alone,
her beauty never seen, unknown,
to mariners of the seven seas,
her golden eyes a mystery.

She waits to hear a siren's song,
through winters, dark, and summers, long,
through cold, dark rain and slashing sleet,
a gentle, soothing cadence, sweet,
a mermaid song that lingers long,
and hoping that their eyes soon meet.

She waits long through the day and night,
through frosty springs and autumns, bright,

to follow close this sea maid song,
this creature from the seven seas,
yearning for that soothing song,
this her wish and only plea,
and from a maiden of the sea.

Hypathia, she sings so softly,
while the twilight's on the waves,
and that is when this golden seahorse
emerges from her silent cave,
and swims to sweet *Hypathia* slowly,
the skies adorned with moonlight, holy.

Upon her back *Hypathia* rides,
with lantern fish along their side.
Across the green-gray waves they glide
and to a place this seahorse knows,
a place where hidden gemstones rest,
where golden treasure, it does glow,
in waters deep, far, far below.